Summary:

The E-Myth Revisited

By: Michael E Gerber

Proudly Brought to you by:

Text Copyright © Readtrepreneur

All rights reserved. No part of this guide may be reproduced in any form without permission in writing from the publisher except in the case of brief quotations embodied in critical articles or reviews.

Legal & Disclaimer

The information contained in this book is not designed to replace or take the place of any form of medicine or professional medical advice. The information in this book has been provided for educational and entertainment purposes only.

The information contained in this book has been compiled from sources deemed reliable, and it is accurate to the best of the Author's knowledge; however, the Author cannot guarantee its accuracy and validity and cannot be held liable for any errors or omissions. Changes are periodically made to this book. You must consult your doctor or get professional medical advice before using any of the suggested remedies, techniques, or information in this book. Images used in this book are not the same as of that of the actual book. This is a totally separate and different entity from that of the original book titled: "The E-Myth Revisited"

Upon using the information contained in this book, you agree to hold harmless the Author from and against any damages, costs, and expenses, including any legal fees potentially resulting from the application of any of the information provided by this guide. This disclaimer applies to any damages or injury caused by the use and application, whether directly or indirectly, of any advice or information presented, whether for breach of contract, tort, negligence, personal injury, criminal intent, or under any other cause of action.

You agree to accept all risks of using the information presented inside this book. You need to consult a professional medical practitioner in order to ensure you are both able and healthy enough to participate in this program.

Table of Contents

The Book at a Glance viii

Foreword xi

Introduction xiii

FREE BONUSES xvi

Part I: 18

The E-Myth and American Small Businesses 18

Chapter 1: The Entrepreneurial Myth 1

Chapter 2: The Entrepreneur, the Manager, and the Technician 3

Chapter 3: Infancy: The Technician's Phase 6

Chapter 4: Adolescence: Getting Some Help 9

Chapter 5: Beyond the Comfort Zone 12

Chapter 6: Maturity and the Entrepreneurial Perspective 15

Part II: 18

The Turn-Key Revolution: A New View of Business 18

Chapter 7: The Turn-Key Revolution 19

Chapter 8: The Franchise Prototype 22

Chapter 9: Working On Your Business, Not In It. 25

Part III: 29

Building a Small Business That Works 29

Chapter 10: The Business Development Process .. 30

Chapter 11: Your Business Development Program 33

Chapter 12: Your Primary Aim 34

Chapter 13: Your Strategic Objective 36

Chapter 14: Your Organizational Strategy 39

Chapter 15: Your Management Strategy 43

Chapter 16: Your People Strategy 46

Chapter 17: Your Marketing Strategy 49

Chapter 18: Your Systems Strategy 52

Epilogue: Bringing the Dream Back to American Small Business 57

Afterword: Taking the First Step 60

Conclusion 61

About the Author 65

FREE BONUSES 66

The Book at a Glance

The E-Myth Revisited is for people who own or want to start a small business. Most small businesses in the United States fail, and the goal of this book is to help you increase the likelihood of achieving success.

Chapter 1 explains the primary reasons why most businesses don't succeed – people go into business with the wrong motivation and fatal assumptions.

Within every potential business owner are three distinct personalities – the Entrepreneur, the Manager, and the Technician, and they are constantly battling against each other. Their different characteristics and how these lead to conflict are discussed in Chapter 2.

All businesses must grow, and Chapter 3 talks about the Infancy phase, when the Technician usually takes over, and why he is not apt to own or lead a business.

Chapter 4 is about the Adolescence phase, when the business owner decides to get some help. It illustrates Management by Abdication, and explains why doing this is harmful to your business.

Chapter 5 describes the three possible directions a business can go when it lacks a Manager – returning to Infancy, going broke, or hanging on for dear life.

For a business to succeed, it must start as a Mature business. Chapter 6 explains how it is done. It also shows the importance of having an Entrepreneurial Perspective.

Chapter 7 is about the Turn-Key Revolution – a way of doing business that has the power to transform small enterprises – through the Business Format Franchise.

Chapter 8 explains what a Franchise Prototype is and how it fulfills the goal of a business owner to give his customers what they want and, at the same time, maintain control of that business.

Chapter 9 shows you how to work on your business and not in it. It also explains the six rules of the franchise game.

Building the Prototype of your business is a continuous process known as the Business Development Process. It is founded on three distinct activities – Innovation, Quantification, and Orchestration – which are described in Chapter 10.

Chapter 11 emphasizes the importance of your Business Development Program.

Chapters 12 to 18 discuss the seven distinct steps included in your Business Development Program: (1) figuring out what your Primary Aim is and its importance in providing your business a direction; (2) developing your Strategic Objective - a clear statement of what your business must do for you in order to achieve your Primary Aim – and understanding the standards that you must set; (3) your Organizational Strategy – the advantage of organizing your company instead of organizing around people, and how to work on prototyping the position in your company; (4) implementing your Management Strategy through a Management System – a marketing tool aiming to produce an effective Prototype; (5) your People Strategy or how you can make them do whatever you want them to; (6) developing your Marketing Strategy by knowing more about your customers; and (7) your Systems Strategy – the three kinds of systems in your business and understanding how they are fully intertwined.

Foreword

It has been 15 years since the first publication of *The E-Myth*. This edition offers clarification of some specific aspects of the E-Myth point of view so that readers can better apply it to their businesses. This book provides answers to many of the questions The E-Myth has raised throughout the years.

Many people wonder what owners of exceptionally successful businesses know that the rest don't. Experience has shown that it's not what these owners know that makes them exceptionally good in business; it's their insatiable craving to know more. The problem with owners of most failing businesses is not that they don't know much about finance, operations, marketing, and management, but that they spend their time and energy upholding what they believe they know. The best of the best are determined to get things right at whatever cost.

On the other hand, successful business owners are exceptionally grounded people. They are obsessed about the little things, realistic, and in touch with the reality of ordinary life. They know that it is the failure to achieve greatness in the things that go on in every nook and cranny of a business that make it miss the mark. The great ones understand that in order to reach something bigger, they must focus their attention on the seemingly insignificant and boring things. The greatest business people are those who have sincere fascination for the impact that little things can have on the world.

This book serves as a guide to those who understand that the growth of an exceptional business is a continuous process. This fascination with growth is not the same as a fascination with the success as we normally think of – reaching an end point that enables someone to say they did it. End points in growth of an exceptional business are immediately replaced by starting points. This book is about beginnings, the exciting process, and the continuous development of our senses and consciousness, which only comes from paying attention to what's going on and being present in the moment.

Introduction

This book was written for people who own or want to own a small business. It represents everything E-Myth Worldwide has done over the past 24 years. It illustrates the belief that small businesses in the United States do not work – a belief that is created and supported by the experiences of their small business owners.

People who own small businesses are working a lot more than they should for the profit they're getting. The problem is that they're doing the wrong work, and this results in a business in chaos.

Statistics show that 80% of small businesses in the United States fail within their first five years. More than 80% of those that survived fail in the second five years.

Why is this the case?

This book presents an answer – four profound ideas. If you understand these, you will have the power to make your business exceptional. Ignore them, and you will probably join the ranks of the failed business owners.

Idea #1. The E-Myth says that small businesses in the United States are founded by entrepreneurs who risk capital to make a profit. However, this is not true, and entrepreneurship has little to do with it.

Idea #2. The Turn-Key Revolution is changing the way we do business, who goes into business, and the odds of survival.

Idea #3. At the heart of the Turn-Key Revolution is the Business Development Process. Applied purposely and systematically, it has the power to transform any small business into an exceptional one.

Idea #4. Any small business owner can apply the Business Development Process in a systematic method integrating the lessons of the Turn-Key Revolution into their operation.

E-Myth Worldwide has helped more than 25,000 small business owners who enrolled in their E-Myth Mastery Program™ since its founding in 1977, all thanks to the implementation of Business Development Process. E-Myth Worldwide has more direct experience utilizing the lessons of the Turn-Key Revolution and the Business Development Process to improve small businesses than any other organization.

This book isn't simply about the "how to's". Books like that don't work. This book focuses on getting results. It is an idea worth working, for that makes people work. The "how to do it" only becomes significant when such an idea becomes incorporated into how a person thinks and operates their business.

This book is about the idea that your business is a reflection of who you are. If your thinking is messy, the way you do business will be sloppy. If you're not organized, your business will be in chaos. If you're greedy, so will your employees be. Hence, if you want your business to change, change must start within you.

FREE BONUSES

P.S. Is it okay if we overdeliver?

Here at Readtrepreneur Publishing, we believe in overdelivering way beyond our reader's expectations. Is it okay if we overdeliver?

Here's the deal, we're going to give you an extremely condensed PDF summary of the book which you've just read and much more…

What's the catch? We need to trust you… You see, we want to overdeliver and in order for us to do that, we've to trust our reader to keep this bonus a secret to themselves? Why? Because we don't want people to be getting our exclusive PDF summaries even without buying our books itself. Unethical, right?

Ok. Are you ready?

Firstly, remember that your book is code: "**READ93**".

Next, visit this link: <http://bit.ly/exclusivepdfs>

Everything else will be self explanatory after you've visited: http://bit.ly/exclusivepdfs.

We hope you'll enjoy our free bonuses as much as we enjoyed preparing it for you!

Part I:

The E-Myth and American Small Businesses

Chapter 1: The Entrepreneurial Myth

There is a belief that small businesses are started by entrepreneurs. This is called the E-Myth. It may be true in rare cases, but not always.

So who are the people who start small businesses in America?

The Entrepreneurial Seizure

To understand this confusion, we should take a closer look at the person who goes into business before they do so.

The truth is that many of these people, like most of those who go into business, started working for somebody else, probably doing technical work. For no obvious reason, something happened. It might have been the weather or the feeling of not being appreciated at work. It doesn't matter what the reason is, but suddenly, they were struck by the *Entrepreneurial Seizure*.

They became obsessed with the thought of being independent, being their own boss, and doing their own thing. It was irresistible and there was no way to get rid of that thought.

They had to start their own business.

The Fatal Assumption

Most people who go into business assume that understanding the technical work involved in a business is the same as understanding the business itself. It's a fatal assumption because the two are completely different. In fact, this belief is the main reason why most small businesses don't succeed.

A technician struck with an *Entrepreneurial Seizure* thinks that a business is where he goes to work. A cook opens up a restaurant. A hair stylist starts a salon. A carpenter becomes a contractor.

What they don't realize is that by starting their own business, their greatest asset becomes their biggest liability. Not knowing how to make the business work, they become someone who does one job really well, and a dozen others that they have no idea to do at all.

Chapter 2: The Entrepreneur, the Manager, and the Technician

A person who starts a business is actually three-people-in-one – the Entrepreneur, Manager, and Technician. The problem is that while each of these personalities wants to be a boss, nobody wants to have a boss. This leads to conflict.

There is a war going on inside every person who owns a small business. It's a three-way battle where, unfortunately, no one can win. To understand why, we have to get to know the differences between the Entrepreneur, Manager, and Technician.

The Entrepreneur

The entrepreneurial personality is the visionary. He turns every condition into an opportunity. He lives in the future and is happiest when he's left free to imagine the "what-if" and "if-when". He's the innovator, crafting new methods to infiltrate and generate new markets.

The Entrepreneur has an exceptional need for control. Living in the future, he must have control of people and actions in the present time in order to focus on his ideas. As an innovator, he desires change. He makes a great deal of chaos, which causes those he includes in his projects to worry.

As a consequence, he often finds himself ahead of others and requiring great effort to pull his followers along. Seeing the world filled with a surplus of opportunities and dragging feet, the Entrepreneur considers most people as problems that only get in the way of his dream.

The Manager

The Manager is practical. Without him, there is no planning and order. In contrast with the Entrepreneur, the managerial personality lives in the past, needs order instead of control, consistently sees problems in events, and instinctively holds on to the status quo.

The Manager organizes and puts in order the things that the Entrepreneur creates. If the Entrepreneur makes a mess, the Manager cleans it up. While the Entrepreneur innovates, the Manager builds a business and society. The tension between the two creates the mixture from which all great work arises.

The Technician

The Technician believes that if you want something done right, you should do it yourself. For him, simply dreaming of things is of no use. Things are supposed to be done.

While the other two live in the future and past, the technical personality thrives in the present – having the ability to feel things and getting them done.

In theory, the Entrepreneur provides him with new and interesting work to do, but the problem is that most of these tasks are not compatible with the real world. For the Technician, the Entrepreneur is just keeping him from doing the things that need to be done by making him work on something new that probably doesn't have to be done at all.

Another problem is the Manager, whom he sees as someone who reduces him to a part of "the system", which for him is dehumanizing and violates his individuality. To the Manager, he is just another problem to manage. For both of them, the Entrepreneur is the one who got them into trouble.

*

Each of us has an Entrepreneur, Manager, and Technician inside us, but unfortunately, the balance among them is rarely achieved. The majority of people who start a small business are 10% Entrepreneur, 20% Manager, and 70% Technician. Clearly, the one in charge is the Technician.

Chapter 3: Infancy: The Technician's Phase

Like people, businesses are supposed to grow, and with it comes change. Unfortunately, most businesses are run according to what the owner wants and not what it needs.

The Technician who gets to run the company wants the opposite. Instead of growth and change, he merely wants a place to go to work free from a boss. This spells doom for the business.

Understanding the three phases of a business's growth is key to discovering why most small businesses fail and making sure that yours thrive.

*

In the beginning, you, as the Technician, think that nothing is too much for your business to ask. You work 10 to 16 hours a day, every single day. Your new business consumes you and you are totally invested in keeping it alive. You're not just doing the work you know how to do, but also the ones that you don't.

In its Infancy, the business and the owner are one. There would be no business if the owner were removed. Therefore, you are the business.

If you're lucky, all your work will begin to pay off soon. Customers are not just coming back, but they're bringing in their friends as well. People keep coming.

Then you'll realize that you're falling behind. More customers means more work to be done than you can handle. Inevitably, the Master Juggler begins to drop some of the balls.

The only thing you can do is to put in more time and energy into your new business. You work at home until late at night, and you need to wake up earlier than usual so you can work immediately. Even on the weekends, when you're supposed to rest your mind, you are busy making sense out of the mess you found yourself in. Yet, you keep on dropping more balls.

Suddenly, you realize that you didn't get rid of your Boss. You only created a new one in the form of your business.

*

Infancy ends when you realize that your business has to change for it to survive. Most business failures take place when this happens. Most of the Technicians walk away from their business. Only the few who didn't, go on to Adolescence.

*

Nothing is wrong with being a Technician. What's wrong is when he owns a business. The entrepreneurial and strategic work – work that the Technician is not doing - is what will lead a business to move forward. When the Technician consumes the other two personalities, he is not building a great small business, but a complicated, unsatisfying, and demeaning job.

If a Technician wants to work in a business, he should work in somebody else's business, and not in his own. Being the doer, he will create a business that can only run with him doing the work. A business that depends on you is not a business. It is a job.

Chapter 4: Adolescence: Getting Some Help

Every business must grow into the Adolescent phase for it to grow. This happens when you decide to get some help.

As a Technician, you will inevitably seek out technical help from someone who has experience in your kind of business, so you hire your first employee.

Enter Harry – a 68-year-old bookkeeper who's been doing the job for 56 years, 22 of those spent in a company just like yours. He knows everything about your kind of business.

Your first morning with Harry – your first employee who would do the work you know nothing about or don't want to do – is a critical time. What will he do when he realizes that you don't know what you're doing? Will he leave or will he do the work?

When you realize he's working, you begin to understand what it means to be in business. The Manager in you takes over. You are free again.

However, you are doing *Management by Abdication* instead of by *Delegation*. Once you hand him the books, you run away. When he's not totally occupied with the books, you give him other tasks. Harry occasionally approaches you to tell you what he needs, but you simply tell him to handle it. It doesn't matter how he does it, as long as he gets it done. Your life then becomes easier.

Your business grows and Harry needs more people. You let him hire them. Harry is reliable and never complains. You get the best of both worlds.

One day, you get calls from customers, bankers, and suppliers complaining about several things. You promise them you'll look into it.

You go to each of your employees whom Harry hired and discover that none of them are doing things right. You tell them to hand you whatever they're doing and that you'll take care of them yourself, and you do.

In every Adolescent business, the process of deterioration begins once the undesirable effects of Management by Abdication surfaces. You and your people's ability to juggle are exceeded by the number of balls in the air. Your balls will fall faster with greater frequency, and it's only the beginning of that process.

Then you realize that you shouldn't have trusted Harry or anyone. The only person who cares about your business is you. If you want things to get done right, you're the one who must do it. To save your business, you become the Master Juggler again.

The owner of an Adolescent business is the one doing everything that has to be done to keep the business running, even when he is paying people who are supposed to do it for him. The more he does, the less they do.

Harry could have told you that the work will never be done to your satisfaction, because as The Boss, you always change your mind about what needs to be done and how it should be done.

What Harry doesn't know is that you're going crazy because you don't know how to do things any other way. For you to act differently, you would need to tap the Entrepreneur and Manager within you.

However, the Technician in you won't let that happen. He has got to go to work and keep busy. He has just stretched the limits of his Comfort Zone.

Chapter 5: Beyond the Comfort Zone

The owner's Comfort Zone is a boundary beyond which they lose their ability to control their environment. Every Adolescent business reaches a point where its owner pushes outside that boundary.

When an owner loses the ability to control his business, he hires a "Harry". But "Harry" is also a technician and needs more guidance than The Technician can provide him. He needs a Manager. The lack of one causes the business to either return to Infancy, go for broke, or hang on for dear life.

Getting Small Again

The Technician-turned-business-owner typically tends to get rid of uncontrollable chaos and returns to Infancy. He gets rid of employees and inventory, rents a smaller facility, and goes back to doing it all by himself again, thereby feeling in control again.

He thinks that by doing so, nothing can go wrong, forgetting that he'd been there before. One day he wakes up not feeling like he wants to go to his business anymore. Then, he realizes that if he doesn't, no one else will. He is again faced with the reality that what he created is not a business but a job.

In the United States, more than 400,000 small businesses close their doors every year.

Going for Broke

Going for broke is a less painful and more dramatic alternative to getting small. In fact, these businesses are a sign of our time.

New technology brings with it a new breed of technicians to the business arena. Most of their businesses grow so fast that their ability to produce their commodity is quickly surpassed by the demand for it.

When a business explodes, the people left behind justify the explosion as an inescapable aftermath of doing business on a fast track, where brilliant technology, luck, and speed are essential to make it big.

The reality is that these three have never been sufficient, because somebody is always better. Unfortunately, there's not enough time to listen once a business goes fast track.

Adolescent Survival

For an Adolescent business, surviving is the most tragic possibility of all.

In order for your business to survive, you have to be fully committed to doing whatever's needed. You do it the way you only know — being there all the time. The business and the possibility of losing it consume you. You dedicate everything you have into it and you manage to keep it going.

In the end, your business doesn't explode. You do. You give everything you have until there's nothing left.

Infancy and Adolescence dominate the American small business. Most of the small businesses visited by E-Myth Worldwide for 24 years were in this condition. Nevertheless, there is a way to escape it.

Chapter 6: Maturity and the Entrepreneurial Perspective

The third phase of a company's growth is maturity. This is exemplified by the greatest businesses in the world.

Maturity is not the inevitable end product of Infancy and Adolescence. The best companies started out that way. The people who launched them had a clear understanding of what they were going into. Although they must go through the first two phases, they go through them in a completely different way.

What makes a person who starts a Mature business is his Entrepreneurial Perspective.

The Entrepreneurial Perspective

According to its founder, Tom Watson, IBM achieved success because of three reasons. First, he had a clear vision of what the company would look like. Next, he had a picture of how IBM would act. Finally, he knew that if they didn't begin to act that way from the start, they would never get there.

It's been decades since Tom Watson talked about the reasons behind his company's success. While IBM is now in trouble and hardly a model for any business owner to follow, it would be different if Watson were still alive. He would have been involved in IBM's reinvention to respond as the future demanded.

*

An Entrepreneurial Perspective takes on a wide and expansive scale. It sees the business as a system of integrated parts that creates a specifically planned result, a systemic way of doing business. There's a standard for the business and it functions in accordance to rules and principles.

In contrast, a Technician's Perspective is narrow and limited. Not seeing the connection between where his business is now and where it is going, he abandons any meaning and higher purpose of his work. Steps are done because of the need to do them. Not having the visionary guidance and larger scale apparent in the Entrepreneurial Model, he is left to build a model based on past experience. This is the exact opposite of what he needs to free himself and the business from work he's been used to doing.

The Entrepreneurial Model

The Entrepreneurial Model is a business model that satisfies the needs of a specific sector of customers in an innovative way. It recognizes that how things are done in a business is more important than what's done.

An Entrepreneurial Model starts with a picture of the customer for whom the business is to be made and not of the business itself. It recognizes that no business can succeed without a clear image of its customers.

On the other hand, The Technician looks at his skills and finds a way to sell them. The result is a business that focuses on what it sells and not the way it is marketed nor the customers to whom the product is sold. Such business is intended to fulfill the owner and not its customers.

So how can we present the Entrepreneurial Model to The Technician in such a way that he can understand and make use of it? Unfortunately, we can't.

What we must do instead is to give the entrepreneur in each of us a business model that is so exhilarating that it inspires our entrepreneurial personality to escape from The Technician's bonds. If the model is to work, The Technician and The Manager need their own models at the same time. It must be balanced and inclusive so that the three personalities find the right work to do.

To find such a model, we should analyze the Turn-Key Revolution.

Part II:

The Turn-Key Revolution: A New View of Business

Chapter 7: The Turn-Key Revolution

Most people are familiar with the Industrial Revolution, Technological Revolution, and Information Explosion and the great impact each has had on our lives. However, only quite a few have ever heard of the Turn-Key Revolution, even though its apparent impact on the future is just as profound.

Put simply, The Turn-Key Revolution is a way of doing business that has the power to transform any small business from a condition of chaos to order and continuous growth.

The Franchise Phenomenon

In 1952, a milkshake machine salesman named Ray Kroc visited the very first MacDonald's hamburger stand. Impressed by the hamburgers and how they were precisely and efficiently made, he convinced Mac and Jim MacDonald to let him franchise their method. 12 years after that, he bought them out and created McDonald's, the world's largest retail prepared food distribution system.

"The Most Successful Small Business in the World"

In less than 40 years, McDonald's has become a $40-billion-a-year business with a global reach and constituting more than 10% of the gross restaurant receipts in America. Kroc created not just a successful business but a model that has built many entrepreneurs their fortunes.

However, franchising itself is not the genius of McDonald's. It's the Business Format Franchise, which has transformed American Business and generated so much of the success of the franchise phenomenon.

Turning the Key: The Business Format Franchise

Franchising has been around even before McDonald's was born, and those businesses were called "trade name" franchises. Small companies were allowed to market the franchisor's nationally known products locally.

The Business Format Franchise is a step ahead because it lends the small company not just the name but a whole system of doing business. It is built on the idea that the true value of a business is not what it sells but how it sells its product. That difference is where the significance and success of the Turn-Key Revolution lies.

Selling the Business Instead of the Product

Ray Kroc was the perfect entrepreneur. He suffered from one big liability just like any typical entrepreneur: he lacked sufficient money to finance his huge dream.

This is where the franchisee came in and facilitated the fulfillment of Kroc's aspiration. At that point, Kroc realized that his product is his business, and his first, last, and most important, customer is the franchisee.

For the franchisee who wanted to buy a business, he only wanted to know if the product worked. For Ray Kroc, making sure that his business would be better than any other was the most significant concern.

Selling his business was not the only reason why Kroc had to make sure that it would work. Given that most small businesses fail, he realized that for McDonald's to succeed, he had to make certain that his business would work once sold and no matter who bought it. Instead of creating a people-dependent business, he built one that is systems-dependent.

That is the secret behind the success of the Business-Format Franchise – the Franchise Prototype. In it is where you can discover the required model to make your business work.

Chapter 8: The Franchise Prototype

The success rate of Business Format Franchises is reported at 95% whereas that of new independently owned businesses is less than 50%. While only 20% of all businesses thrive in their first five years, 75% of all Business Format Franchises succeed. This success is attributed to the Franchise Prototype.

The Franchise Prototype is where all assumptions are tested to determine how well they work before being operated in the business. Without it, the franchise would be as chaotic and disorderly as any other business.

In a Franchise Prototype, people run the system, which runs the business. The system incorporates all the factors required to solve the problems that keep a business from working well. It converts the business into a machine that is powered by the integrity of its components.

At McDonald's, they tested every possible detail of the system in the Prototype, and then controlled these to an extent that had never been reached in a people-intensive business. The system guarantees the fulfillment of a customer's expectations in exactly the same way every single time. It is important for Kroc that the customers don't equate inexpensive with cheap.

To ensure this, a franchisee is first sent to a rigorous training program before being allowed to run the franchise. This leaves the franchisee with little to no room for making changes in the operation. Only when he learns the system is he handed the key to his own business. Hence the name Turn-Key Operation.

Franchisees love this model. All they have to do is buy the right to use the system and learn how to operate it and the business does the rest. With a system that has been perfected by the franchisor, all they need is to manage it.

A business owner's goal is to give their customers exactly what they want and, at the same time, maintain control of the business that's handing it to them. The Franchise Prototype is the solution for that.

The Franchise Prototype provides The Entrepreneur a channel through which his vision materializes in the real world. It offers The Manager his much needed order, certainty, and system. To The Technician, it creates a place where he can do the technical work that he loves so much. Finally, it provides an individual the means to satisfy the three personalities within them while building a business that works.

As a small business owner, this is what you've been looking

for. It definitely works and it's been there all along. It's been there at McDonald's, Subway Sandwiches, Kentucky Fried Chicken, Taco Bell, Pizza Hut, UPS, Disney World, and Universal Studios.

What ultimately differentiates every exceptional business from every single one of its competitors is its proprietary way of doing business. Franchised or not, a Proprietary Operating System is at the heart of these extraordinary businesses.

Now, how do you build your own Franchise Prototype? How do you create a business that can run even without you? How do you free yourself from your business?

Chapter 9: Working On Your Business, Not In It

Your life should not be all about your business. These two are entirely different things and rather than being a part of you, your business should be apart from you. Recognize that the main purpose of your business is to serve your life and not the other way around.

You can benefit from the Franchise Prototype model when you want to work on your business and not in it. Think of your business, or one that you want to own, as a prototype of thousands more. If you pretend that it's a business for franchise, you already know the game.

Since every game imposes rules, let's look at the rules of the franchise game.

1. The Model Will Provide Consistent Value to Your Customers, Employees, Suppliers, and Lenders, Beyond What They Expect

Value can be the words uttered to a customer as they leave. It can be a gesture of appreciation to an employee for a job well done. It can be a simple "thank you" to your banker for their dependability. It can be a surprise gift from the business. It can be the enthusiasm you show in explaining your product to a customer. In short, value is what people recognize it to be.

Value is important to your business and to the fulfillment it gives you as it grows.

2. The Model Will Be Operated by People with the Lowest Possible Level of Skills

If your model is designed for highly-skilled individuals, it will be impossible to replicate. Such people are also expensive, so you will have to increase the price of your product or service.

Of course, if you have a law firm, you need lawyers. What it refers to is the lowest possible level required to accomplish the functions for which each model is aimed at. Your goal is to build a system where ordinary people can produce superb results.

3. The Model Will Stand Out as a Place of Impeccable Order

In a world where chaos dominates, most people want order. An organized business gives its customers and its employees relatively fixed points of reference much needed in a chaotic world.

A well-organized business tells your customers that your employees know what they're doing and assures your employees that you yourself know what you're doing. A well-organized business tells your customers that you can be trusted to deliver desired results, and your employees that they can entrust their future with you.

4. All Work in the Model Will Be Documented in Operations Manuals

Without documentation, your people will not have the clear structure they need. Documentation shows them a written account of how the job is done. It communicates to the new employees that there is some meaning in the world they have chosen to work. It gives you the ability to make clear demands on their time and energy.

The Operations Manual is the warehouse of your documentation. It defines the work's objective, lays down the steps required to do a specific work, and summarizes the standards related to the process and result.

5. The Model Will Provide a Uniformly Predictable Service to the Customer

A business must not only look orderly but also act that way in order to function predictably and uniformly. Most customers prefer to have a control of their experience. They want to know what to expect.

Knowing your business, having affable and efficient employees, and delivering excellent results will matter much less if you don't provide a consistent experience to your customers. Expectations are created during the first meeting with your customers, and if their expectations are not met when they return, you will easily lose them.

You can't give your customer a wonderful experience and then suddenly take it away. Remember that they can always go somewhere else.

6. The Model Will Utilize a Uniform Color, Dress, and Facilities Code

Consumer decisions are influenced by the shapes and colors they find in the marketplace. Therefore, your model's shape and color can make or break your business.

There are colors and shapes that work for your business and there are those that don't. The colors and shapes you show your customers should be scientifically identified and employed throughout your model. Consider your model as a package for your sole product – your business.

Part III:

Building a Small Business That Works

Chapter 10: The Business Development Process

The continuous process of building the Prototype of your business is called the Business Development Process. It is founded on Innovation, Quantification, and Orchestration.

Innovation

Innovation is often equated to creativity. Creativity is limited to thinking about getting things done, while innovation is actually getting things done.

Recognizing that the business is the product, franchisors are able to divert their innovative energy from the commodity to the process by which it is created and sold. To them, how they do business is a marketing tool for finding and keeping customers.

Innovation is the core of every exceptionally successful business. For it to be meaningful, it must see through the eyes of the customers. It should also make things easier for the owner and the people involved in the operation of the business.

Innovation constantly asks what's standing in the way of customers getting what they want and how to do things better.

Quantification

To be effective and to determine whether it works, Innovation should be quantified. This means that the numbers associated to the impact an innovation creates should be determined.

If you are told that by changing the words your employees use to greet a customer your sales can increase by 16%, the only way to know is to quantify. This involves determining the number of people that came in the door and that actually purchased your product both before and after the change was put into effect. These numbers help you identify the value of your Innovation.

Unfortunately, most businesses do not employ Quantification, and this costs them a fortune. Only a few small business owners think that such seemingly irrelevant Innovation have significance. However, if you could achieve a 10% increase in sales by doing little things like wearing a blue suit instead of black, would you do it?

Quantify everything that is associated to how you do business – from the numbers of customers you see in person each day to the number of products sold each week. Quantify everything and ultimately, you and your employees will see your business in terms of the numbers. With these, you'll know where your business is and where it is going.

Orchestration

Once you're done with innovation and quantification and once you've discovered something that works better than what came before it, you will have to orchestrate the whole thing. You should eliminate discretion at the operating level of your business. If everyone in your business is doing things differently, you're creating chaos instead of order.

If wearing a blue suit or saying a specific thing works, do it every single time. Every person who started every exceptional Business Format Franchise company knows that you don't own something that you haven't orchestrated.

Orchestration is persistently doing what you do for as long as it creates the results that you want. Once it doesn't, change it. The Business Development Process is dynamic. Innovation, quantification, and orchestration should be a continuous process because the world will not tolerate a static object.

Chapter 11: Your Business Development Program

Now it is clear to you what your agenda should be: to consider your business as a prototype for thousands more exactly like it.

Imagine that someone will buy your business, but only if it works without so much work, and even without you.

Imagine yourself explaining to a potential buyer every component of your business and how it works and how you've incorporated the process of innovation, quantification, and orchestration in your business. Imagine yourself introducing them to your people and how impressed they would be with the order and predictability of your system.

Your Business Development Program is the process that will transform your envisioned or existing business into a perfect prototype for thousands more. Through this program, you will be able to build your Franchise Prototype.

The Program consists of seven steps, which will be discussed in the next seven chapters.

Chapter 12: Your Primary Aim

While your business can play a significant role in your life, we already know that it shouldn't be your life and so it must not be the first order of business on our agenda. You are.

In this life, what is the most important to you? How do you want to live your life?

Your answer to all these questions is your Primary Aim. Once you've figured this out, you need to actively make your life into what you wish it to be. It's simple but it's not going to be easy.

If you want your business to achieve any meaning other than work, it's imperative to recognize what your aim is. Your business can only make a huge contribution to the realization of your dream if it knows what your aim is.

By recognizing what your Primary Aim is, you can begin to live it. You'll figure out what steps to take and be able to measure your progress. You'll know where you were, how far you've gone, and how much farther you still have to go. Without a Primary Aim, it will be virtually impossible to know this. Your life will just drift without any direction and be without purpose and meaning.

Like Mature companies, great persons are aware how they are able to reach their current status and what they must accomplish to get to where they want to be. They have in their mind a picture of the life they want and spend their lives every single day living out the vision they have. They determine if there's a disparity between what they've done and what they aimed to do, and if there is, they immediately work on making up the difference.

The difference between great persons and those who aren't is that the former actively build their lives, while the latter is a product of their lives, letting life take its course. Great people live fully while everyone else merely exists. Great people live intentionally while everyone else lives by accident.

Your Primary Aim is what can make you bring your business to life. It gives you energy, purpose, and the grist for your day-to-day mill.

Chapter 13: Your Strategic Objective

Once you determine your Primary Aim, you can then start developing your Strategic Objective – a clear statement of what your business must do for you in order to achieve your Primary Aim.

Your Strategic Objective is the product of your Life Plan and Business Strategy and Plan. Your Life Plan outlines your life and business. Your Business Strategy and Plan provide the structure to your business operation in order for it to fulfill your Life Plan. It is also valuable in promoting your business to your banker, investors, and strategic ties in the business community.

For your Business Strategy and Plan to work, it should be trimmed down into a list of simple and clear standards. Such a list of standards is your Strategic Objective.

The First Standard: Money

Gross revenues. Gross profits. Pretax profits. After-tax profits. You can't know all these numbers that far in the future. However, it doesn't matter, because when you're just starting, any standards are better than none at all.

The first thing that you must always determine is what will

serve your Primary Aim. In terms of money, you should identify how much you will need to live independent of work. In fact, the sole reason for creating your own business is selling it. You'll be able to because it works. You built it that way so that it can give you and your buyer whatever both of you want.

The Second Standard: An Opportunity Worth Pursuing

Once you've identified what the first standard should be, you should determine whether your business has a realistic chance of fulfilling those standards. If you find reasons to assume that it can, then it is worth pursuing. No matter how exciting and appealing it is, if you can't find a reason, walk away from it. It will only eat much of your time and keep you from finding the one that is worth pursuing.

A business worth pursuing is one that can ease a frustration felt by a consumer group that is large enough. By knowing this, you have already satisfied the two main requirements of your Strategic Objective – recognizing what you need to sell and to whom.

Standards Three Through?

The Strategic Objective does not have a specific number of standards. Nevertheless, you must have an answer to these specific questions:

- How long will it take for your Prototype to be completed?

- What is the reach of your business? Is it staying local or do you plan for it to go international?

- Will your business be retail, wholesale, or a combination of both?

- What standards will you impose when it comes to cleanliness, clothing, reporting, management, hiring, training, firing, and so forth?

The standards you construct for your business will outline not only your business but also the experience you will have. Your standards create the future model of your business. It supplies the energy by which extraordinary businesses and the most valuable people generate results.

Chapter 14: Your Organizational Strategy

If you want your business to be organized, start by creating an Organization Chart. The organizational development indicated in this chart can have greater impact on a small company than any other Business Development step.

Organizing Around Personalities

Most companies organize around people rather than responsibilities, and this almost always results in chaos. To best illustrate this, let's take a look at Jack and Murray's new company called Widget Makers.

When the brothers started the company, they were sure that it would make them rich. As partners, they share the work between them. When Murray's not attending to the customers, Jack is. When Murray's not making the widget, Jack is. The business is running smoothly, the shop is perfect, and the customers are satisfied.

The brothers go on that way and the business starts to grow. Eventually, work piles up because it is too much for them to handle. They need help, so they hire their nephew, Jerry. They think that if they have to pay someone, it's better to keep it in the family.

Now it's the three of them taking turns. Business continues to grow and they find themselves not able to keep up with the tasks. They eventually hire Herb, Jack and Murray's cousin. He is hardworking, eager, and willing.

Now it's the four of them taking turns. Suddenly, problems come up. Widgets are not working. The shop is unkempt and tools keep getting misplaced. Tensions begin to rise. Jack wants to say something but he's not sure what or to whom. Murray feels the same thing. No one is given a specific responsibility, so none of them is accountable for anything.

Without an Organization Chart, you will have to rely on luck, good feelings, and the goodwill shared by you and your people. These things alone can only lead to chaos and disaster. Organization requires more.

Organizing Your Company

Let's recreate Widget Makers. To make sure that it succeeds, the brothers consider their business as a corporation and not a partnership. Jack and Murray are shareholders and not partners. They are aware that nothing can be worse than a partnership that's also a family business. To save them a lot of trouble later on, Jack and Murray agree that their role outside of the business is shareholders, while inside, they will think of themselves as employees.

Their next step is the creation of a Strategic Objective for Widget Makers. Murray conducts the needed research relating to the Central Demographic Model they have initially picked. Jack organizes the financial data required to secure a loan from the bank. The results they gather are encouraging so they continue to complete their Strategic Objective and start forming the Organization Chart. With the Strategic Objective indicating how they will be doing business, they come up with the necessary positions that must be included in the Organization Chart.

Even though only their names will fill out the chart, the two create a Position Contract for every position on their chart. This is different from a job description because a contract provides a sense of commitment and accountability to each person in an organization. Once they agree on who takes each position, the organization is complete. By building an Organization Chart, they create the blueprint for their Franchise Prototype.

Prototyping the Position: Replacing Yourself with a System

Jack and Murray begin the process of prototyping from the bottom. If their business is going to succeed, they have to find technicians to do the Tactical Work so as to free themselves – the managers – to do the Strategic Work.

The brothers go to work in their business focused on creating a business that works. As Jack goes to work as Salesperson, he also applies Innovation, Quantification, and Orchestration to ultimately come up with a Widget Makers Sales Operations Manual. Only when this is complete does Jack hire the right salesperson – someone who is a novice and is open to the possibility of learning new skills. Murray does the same thing for each of the Tactical Work positions he's accountable for. Eventually, Jack and Murray acquire freedom from the other work and become engaged in Strategic Work.

Chapter 15: Your Management Strategy

Successfully implementing a management strategy doesn't depend on finding exceptionally competent managers. What you must have is Management System.

What Is a Management System?

It's a system through which your Prototype produces a marketing result. For your Franchise Prototype to be more effective, your system should be more automated. The process of building your Management System is a marketing tool. Its aim is to produce an effective Prototype – a business that attracts and produces loyal customers better than any other while making a good profit.

Let's examine how that kind of system was applied by a resort hotel Michael has frequented over the past 17 years.

A Match, a Mint, a Cup of Coffee, and a Newspaper

The first time Michael spent a night in Venetia Hotel, he didn't plan to go there. He was tired from driving all day and needed a place to rest. The moment he walked into the lobby, he felt that he was in a special place.

Despite having no reservation, Michael noted that it took no more than three minutes from the moment he was greeted by the woman behind the front desk to the time he was escorted by the bellboy to his room. When he went to the restaurant, he was delighted to find out that the woman had made him a dinner reservation while she was checking him in.

The night had turned chilly by the time he got back to his room. Looking forward to a fire and another brandy, he was pleased to find the fireplace already lit, the quilt turned down on the bed, and the pillows plumped up with a mint placed on each one. There was also a glass of brandy on one of the tables beside the bed.

He woke up the next day to the sound of coffee bubbling in its pot, automatically turned on by a timer. He was surprised to find that it was his brand of coffee, and then realized that he was asked what brand he preferred at the restaurant the night before. When he opened his door, he found on the mat the newspaper he preferred. That amazed him as well, and then he remembered the receptionist asking him his preferred newspaper when he was checking in.

Every time he has returned to that hotel, exactly the same scenario has occurred. Except that they never asked his preferences again. Michael had become part of its Management System, providing him exactly what he wants, the same way, every single time.

Curious about how the hotel consistently delivered the same experience, Michael talked with the Manager after his third visit. The Manager showed him their very detailed Operations Manual, which was nothing but a series of checklists. He explained that each of them was completed by their personnel to verify that each responsibility was done according to the standards. In addition, they had an effective automated system that ensured delivery of predictable results to the guests. The Manager pointed out that everything in the hotel was put together such that it would make a positive impression on their guests.

Chapter 16: Your People Strategy

You can't make people do everything you want them to do, but you can develop an environment where your people believe that "doing it" is a lot more important than not.

How does the Manager of Venetia Hotel get his people do what he wants? The hotel's owner takes the business operation very seriously and makes sure that his people are aware of it. At the same time, he treats them seriously and makes them realize that they are important and that their job is important to him. He makes sure that the people who work for him understand the idea behind their delegated tasks, which is more important than the work itself.

Given a choice, people will prefer to work for someone who has built clearly defined structures where they can put themselves to the test. It's like a game where the rules represent the idea you have about the world. Getting people to do things you want them to is like getting them to play your game by communicating the game to them.

The Rules of the Game

If you want to become good at the "people game", the rules you set must be honored. Some of these rules are listed below but you'll have to discover the rest of them by playing your own game.

1. If you want your employees to take the game seriously, it must come first before figuring out what you want your people to do.

2. Make sure that you're willing to play the game you create for your people.

3. Change the tactics of your game from time to time but never the strategy. Observe your people to know if it's time for a change.

4. Note that your game is never self-sustaining so you must remind your people of it regularly. People have the tendency to forget and be distracted, which can lead to the loss of your game.

5. Your game must have logic and should be built on universally verifiable truths. Logic gives your people reason to commit to the game.

6. It's okay to "borrow" someone else's game if you can't come up with a good one for yourself. However, if you do borrow someone else's game, you must learn the game by heart.

The Logic of the Game

The hotel Manager saw that the owner's game was simple but effective, so he learned how to play it. The game was developed on the following logic:

These days, most people are not getting what they want, and part of what they're missing is a *Game Worth Playing* and a sense of relationship. As a consequence, most of us seek distraction in things to which we can bestow meaning and significance. What we need, then, is a place where there is order, purpose, and meaning. That's exactly what a business can do.

Playing the Game

Think of the way the hotel owner did and built a business with profound dedication to the idea of providing his customers with great satisfaction. Then, communicate this idea to your people, both in word and deed, through a well-designed process. The hotel owner accomplished this through documented systems and his positive and encouraging manner. Remember that the best method to communicate the systematic yet human process of satisfying customers to your people is to communicate it to them in a systematic and human way. Hence, the way of communication is just as significant as the idea it was meant to communicate.

Chapter 17: Your Marketing Strategy

When developing your Marketing Strategy, besides your customer, forget everything else. When it comes to marketing, what matters is what your customer wants, not you. What you think they want is most likely substantially different from what they actually want.

The Irrational Decision Maker

The first step in a customer's buying process is data gathering. They take in all the information they utilize to decide whether to buy or not.

Your customer's Conscious Mind gathers the information needed to come up with a decision. Although it is actively absorbing data, it is unaware of most of them because what it does is mostly unconscious; that is automatic and habitual.

The second step of the buying process takes place in the Unconscious Mind. Here lie your customer's expectations, which stem from the accumulation of all their experiences. These expectations are fed with food in the form of information coming from the Conscious Mind. The Unconscious Mind says "yes" if the food is compatible with the expectation. Otherwise, it says "no". The decision is made instantly as it gets a taste.

Remember that decisions are made unconsciously and instantly. In fact, your customer has already come up with a decision before you even meet. They just don't know it.

The Two Pillars of a Successful Marketing Strategy

You can only know what your customer wants if you know their demographics and their psychographics. These two are the essential pillars sustaining a successful marketing program.

Demographics tell you who your customer is and psychographics help you determine why they buy. Knowing these two, you can start building a Prototype to fulfill their unconscious needs.

Imagine a person wearing a navy blue suit. Do they look dependable and reliable? Your answer must be yes. In fact, research shows that it's the most powerful suit a person can wear in business.

Now, imagine the same person wearing an orange suit instead. How do you feel about them now? You must think they are the exact opposite of the person wearing a navy suit.

It's important to know that the difference between the two is all in your mind. This difference is perceived instantaneously without even giving it a thought. When it comes to your business, what you should look for doesn't have to be an actual need but a perceived one, and fill that need.

Even if your customer has an actual need, they will not know it if they don't perceive they need something. Such perception is at the core of their decision-making process.

By knowing a customer's demographics, you can recognize their perceptions, and then discover how to satisfy these perceptions and the expectations they create. You can understand their psychographic reality.

Chapter 18: Your Systems Strategy

A system is a group of information, ideas, actions, and things that work together, and in so doing, modify other systems. Therefore, everything is a system.

Let's take a look at the systems in your business.

Three Kinds of Systems

The three kinds of systems in your business are Hard, Soft, and Information.

Hard Systems are the inanimate, non-living things. Your computer and the colors in your shop or office are all part of the Hard System.

Soft Systems are either living things or ideas. You are part of the Soft System.

Information Systems are the things that communicate to us the interaction between the other two. Inventory control and sales activity summary reports are Information Systems.

Your Business Development Program is all about the Innovation, Quantification, Orchestration, and integration of these three kinds of systems. Below are examples of how each of these systems integrate to generate a desirable result.

Hard Systems

At E-Myth Worldwide, white boards used to be extensively used in seminars, meetings, and conferences. During that time, color standards dictated that they used white boards and blue markers. It also imposed that walls should be white. Soon, conflict evolved between standards of cleanliness and color standards.

Cleaning the board-work was not a favorite job among employees. In the haste of getting it done to do the things they preferred to do, they would often glide the eraser uncontrollably over the board's edge, staining the white walls with blue smudge.

To address this, Board Cleaning Policies and Cleaning Teams were created, and signs reminding everyone to be careful were installed, but it didn't solve the problem. Going back to black boards and white chalk or painting the walls white over and over again wasn't acceptable.

The company had conflicting standards. What they wanted was conflicting with what they had. That was an essential condition for innovation, which gave birth to a system. However, the will that they had to solve the problem was what ultimately created the solution. That's how their

Prevent-a-Smudge System was born. By installing Lucite collar around each board, the blue smudges were never a problem again. A Hard System freed their employees to do the things they wanted to do.

Soft Systems

Products need to be sold, and it's typically the people who do that. There's a saying in business that 80% of sales are created by 20% of the people. The difference is that 20% use a system while 80% don't.

A system used for selling is a Soft System. A selling system is an entirely orchestrated interaction between you and your customer. It follows six primary steps:

1. Identify the consumer decision points or Benchmarks in your selling process.

2. Record the words that will get you to each one successfully. Write them down like the script for a play.

3. Create different materials that will be used with each script.

4. Memorize each Benchmark's script.

5. Make sure that your salespeople deliver each script in the same fashion.

6. Assure that your people can communicate effectively. Make sure that they articulate, watch, listen, hear, acknowledge, understand, and engage every prospect as fully as they need to be.

Information Systems

Information should be recorded either manually or as database on your computer. In the Selling System example, the Information System will track its activity from Benchmark to Benchmark. It can tell you an astounding number of things. For instance, it can show you at which Benchmark salespersons may need help. The Information System can tell you what you need to know in order to improve, control, and modify your Selling System or your Finance and Production and Product Development.

*

The systems in your business are fully intertwined. Separating them from one another is difficult. That's why it is necessary for you to see your business as a fully integrated system where everything affects everything else.

Your Primary Aim, Strategic Objective, Organizational Strategy, Management Strategy, People Strategy, Marketing Strategy, and Systems Strategy are all completely interdependent. The success of your Business Development Program entirely depends on your understanding of that integration. That integration is your Prototype.

Epilogue: Bringing the Dream Back to American Small Business

This book is not just a prescription for success, but also a call to learning – how to feel, think, and act differently, more effectively, and more humanly than our existing skills.

Geographic, political, social, and emotional boundaries that once served us no longer exist. The world is constantly changing, which results in chaos, disorder, and trouble.

We don't have to change the world out there. We can't. If we're to succeed, we must change *here*. In reality, we are the ones who are in chaos, not the world. The chaos that we perceive is only a reflection of our inner turmoil. If we want to change the world, that change must begin within our lives.

Bridging the Gap

This book aims to bridge the gap between the world out there and the one in here. Your business can serve as that bridge between the world and you in such a way that makes both more human, more productive, and both worlds work.

A small business, like yours, is a place where we can execute ideas that can change lives. It is a place where rules must be adhered to and order upheld. It is a place that is practical and not idealistic. It is a world small enough to be manageable and responsive but big enough to examine everything we have. A small business is a world of our own.

A World of Our Own

The dream for many American small businesses is to build a world of their own. Millions are going into business to flee the world of chaos. It is a means to create structure, form, control, and a relationship with ourselves and the world, which are impossible to experience in a job.

Unfortunately, this dream is rarely realized because we carry chaos with us. We try to change the world, but we resist change within ourselves, so the small business turns into the worst job in the world.

To change our lives and build a world of our own, we must understand how such a world is built, how it functions, and the rules of the game. We must study the small business that we have, and we can do it effectively with a Business Development Program. The Franchise Prototype can give our study the order it requires to succeed.

An Idea for Action

Does the model of the Franchise Prototype work for you?

Your model works because it demands the complete engagement of the people working it. It can't be done in any other way. The Process of Business Development generates immediate change in the people who participate in it.

In order to continue the process, those who engage in it must not forget their aim. By remembering, their aim becomes fastened to their business where aims can be tested in a concrete way. The business becomes a manifestation of the life they wish to live.

Stop thinking about it. It's time for you to act. Unless you do so, your idea will be nothing but a creative thought. Turn it into an innovation and Bring the Dream Back to American Small Business.

Afterword: Taking the First Step

Now that you want to get started and turn your business into a turn-key operation, you must take the first step.

Look at your business through your new E-Myth eyes. Examine your business as it is now, decide how exactly you want it, and determine the gap between your dream and your current reality. That gap will show you what you must do to build the business of your dreams. Using your E-Myth eyes, you will find out that the gap always comes from the lack of systems.

Since E-Myth has appeared in 1986, it has helped thousands of small-business owners to discover what the gap was in each of their cases, and it would love to do the same for you. Take part in the free E-Myth experience and find out how to get from where you are to where you want to be.

Conclusion

Most small businesses in America fail because they are started by people who are struck by an Entrepreneurial Seizure. The majority of these persons are Technicians who assume that understanding the technical aspect of a business is the same as understanding how to run a business.

The key to succeeding is to start a Mature business – one that knows how it got to where it is and what it needs to do in order to get to where it wants to go. For a person to launch a Mature business, they must have an Entrepreneurial Perspective. They must have the ability to see their business as a system of integrated parts that creates a systemic way of doing business.

The Turn-Key Revolution has the power to transform any small business from a state of chaos to order and continuous growth. Fundamental to this is the Business Format Franchise, which is built on the idea that the true value of a business lies not on the product it sells but on how these products are sold. In fact, it has a success rate of 90%.

The secret behind the success of the Business Format Franchise is the Franchise Prototype – a system that provides the Entrepreneur a medium to realize his vision, the Manager

CONCLUSION

the order he so desires, and the Technician a place where he can do technical work. It satisfies the three personalities within an individual while building a business that works.

In building your own Prototype, you must adhere to the six rules of the franchise game:

1. Your model must provide your customers, employees, bankers, and lenders value that is both consistent and beyond what they expect.

2. Your model must be operated by people with the lowest possible level of skills required to accomplish the functions for which each model is aimed at.

3. Your model must be a place of total order.

4. You must document all work in the model in an Operations Manual.

5. Your model must provide your customer a uniform and predictable service.

6. Your model must use a uniform color, dress, and facilities code.

The Business Development Process is founded on Innovation, Quantification, and Orchestration. Innovation is about getting things done and constantly asking how to do things better in order to provide the customers what exactly they want. Quantification is needed to determine whether the

Innovation works. The numbers associated to the impact an innovation generates should be identified. Finally, Orchestration is persistently doing what you do for as long as it creates the results that you want.

Your Business Development Program is the medium through which you can build your Franchise Prototype. This program consists of seven distinct steps.

1. Figure out what your Primary Aim is to determine what steps you should take and be able to measure your progress. Great people live their lives intentionally while others live by accident.

2. Develop your Strategic Objective. You must have a clear statement of what your business must do for you. The first standard is money – the amount you need to live independent of work. The second is that your business must be an opportunity that is worth pursuing. It should have a realistic chance of fulfilling your standards.

3. Create an Organization Chart, but don't organize around people. It can only lead to chaos and disaster. Organize based on the positions in your company. Prototype these positions but begin at the bottom. Free yourself from the Tactical Work so that you can

focus on the Strategic Work.

4. Use a Management System to successfully implement your management strategy. Your system should be more automated for your Franchise Prototype to be more effective.

5. Because it's impossible to have a full command of people, you must create an environment where your people believe that doing everything you want them to do is a lot better than not doing it. Make the people who work for you understand the idea behind the work they're asked to do, which is more important than the work itself.

6. In developing your Marketing Strategy, remember that what matters most is what your customers want. To identify what they want, you must know their demographics and psychographics. Demographics tell you who your customer is and psychographics help you understand why certain demographic types buy for one reason while others buy for another.

7. Finally, understand that everything in your business is part of a system. It is either a Hard System, Soft System, or Information System. Everything that happens in one system affects everything else.

About the Author

Michael E. Gerber is the Founder, Chairman, and CEO of E-Myth Worldwide, a company established to help small-business owners build a business that works. Since 1977, it has helped more than 25,000 small and emerging business-owner clients. He is regarded by many as "the leading voice of small-business in America".

FREE BONUSES

P.S. Is it okay if we overdeliver?

Here at Readtrepreneur Publishing, we believe in overdelivering way beyond our reader's expectations. Is it okay if we overdeliver?

Here's the deal, we're going to give you an extremely condensed PDF summary of the book which you've just read and much more…

What's the catch? We need to trust you… You see, we want to overdeliver and in order for us to do that, we've to trust our reader to keep this bonus a secret to themselves? Why? Because we don't want people to be getting our exclusive PDF summaries even without buying our books itself. Unethical, right?

Ok. Are you ready?

Firstly, remember that your book is code: "**READ93**".

Next, visit this link: http://bit.ly/exclusivepdfs

Everything else will be self explanatory after you've visited: http://bit.ly/exclusivepdfs.

We hope you'll enjoy our free bonuses as much as we enjoyed preparing it for you!